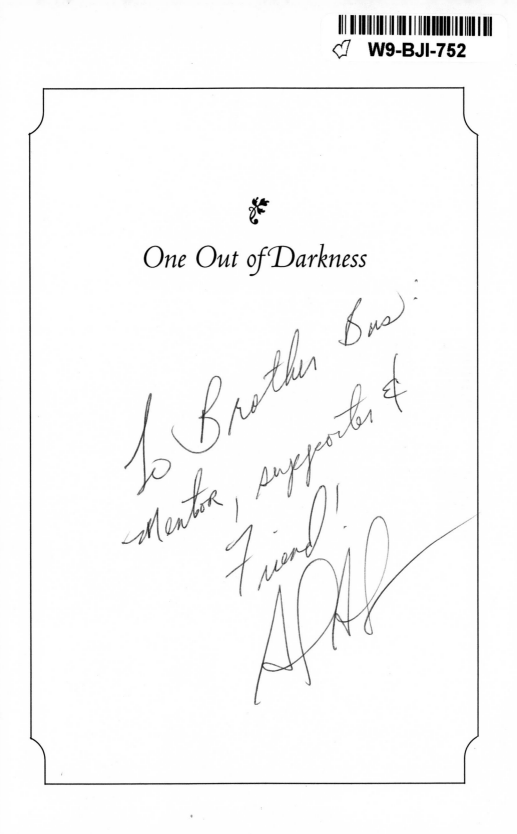

One Out of Darkness

To Brother Bus:

mentor, supporter &

Friend!

One Out of Darkness

Poems of a DC Brother

Stan Stewart

iUniverse, Inc.
New York Lincoln Shanghai

One Out of Darkness
Poems of a DC Brother

Copyright © 2007 by Stan Stewart

iUniverse books may be ordered through booksellers or by contacting:

iUniverse
2021 Pine Lake Road, Suite 100
Lincoln, NE 68512
www.iuniverse.com
1-800-Authors (1-800-288-4677)

ISBN: 978-0-595-42757-4 (pbk)
ISBN: 978-0-595-68143-3 (cloth)
ISBN: 978-0-595-87087-5 (ebk)

Printed in the United States of America

Contents

Introduction

One Out of Darkness: Poems of a DC Brother, expresses some of the experiences I have had, as an African American from Washington, DC, growing from boy to man. These works represent three of the major themes in my life; Inspirational; things which have inspired me, Heritage, reflections upon my heritage as an African American, and Love, which I believe to be the most powerful and positive element known to exist.

In terms of Inspiration, some of the experiences I have had have included things which have broken and even destroyed others. Not saying that I am stronger, better, per se, but quite the contrary; I've been left with a survivor's guilt of sorts, i.e., wondering why I was able to make it through these storms that felled many whom I thought to be wiser, stronger, than I. And so I gained inspiration from these, my fallen brothers and sisters, hoping to use their lessons to avoid their mistakes. And hoping to inspire others through these works, wherein I openly and candidly speak exactly what is in my heart as to the things that continue to inspire and encourage me.

The Heritage section differs in that therein, I attempt to speak of the ancestral inheritance that African Americans possess, but few seem aware of or willing to acknowledge. Someone once wrote that what is past is prologue and this statement, to me, validates that all peoples must know of their origins so as to understand their present circumstances and develop their future-oriented strategies for improving their conditions and preparing for those that will surely follow them.

Finally, I address Love and some of my interpretations and understandings and experiences with this, the greatest of all phenomena in the universe. Speaking in terms of the heart's language and acknowledging passions' importance in relationships.

Thank you for the opportunity to present One Out of Darkness: Poems of a DC Brother.

Peace & Love,

Stan Stewart

Inspirational Section

Soul of the Muse

Would but a little bit of me and my essence
be made known to them and make a presence.

Spreading out across the air—
wouldn't that be something? Do you think they'd care?

It would blow their minds, in time. It would blow their minds.

The soul of the muse being free, you see,
the essence of my iconoclastic presence in this society.

Telling folks things that they already should know—
the truth about the emperor's new clothes.

It would blow their minds, in time. It would blow their minds.

I Carry with Me

Everyone I have known and all that I have experienced, I carry inside of me.
The proper and the strong, the bad and the ugly.

The light and the darkness coexisting somehow.
The past and the present, the then and the now.

And I carry them with me.

My boy, Tiago, dying in the fire at five.
Damon getting shot on Monroe playground, seeing a man approaching death
and his last moments of being alive.

The scent of my momma's cooking and the warmth of my lady's embrace.
The laughter of my children and their kisses on their Poppy's face.

And I carry them with me.
Street footballer and thug to tuba player in a marching band.
From a runaway child to a scholar and Renaissance Man.

The Reason You Upset Them

Since you asked, I'll tell you why.

What you give them is too precious for them to accept,
Too pure for them to understand.
Yours is a Light in the shadows, a refuge in a barren land.

They've been put down and pushed under for so long,
That knowing someone like you exists,
to them seems wrong.

Here I Stand

Upon the convictions of fairness and equality, here I stand.
This former street soldier now a Renaissance Man.

I make the most of my time in this space to speak truth.
My lifestyle and words as my witnesses, my proof.

Admitting at the outset that perfection in me cannot be attained.
Nevertheless still striving to appreciate what God has allowed me to gain.

Knowing that the positions I take are sometimes a dare.
Saying what I am compelled to speak, my soul's voice laid bare.

I stand.

A Man.

I, Stan.

How Could You Dare?

You'd no right to take me there.
I would have been content to sit in life's easy chair,
eyes glazing over with a nonchalant stare.
How could you dare?

Speaking to me, to my essence, to my soul,
with your soft voice and stories so bold.
Sharing with me ancient wisdoms well told.

You had to have known, you must've knew,
how my spirit would respond to your soul's wisdom, didn't you?
You felt me, you felt my essence, taking this mature man back to the charms of
adolescence.

You awakened my muse.
You sparked a poet's fuse!

And now I help carry the iconoclastic banner,
hitting the truth with the Divine's hammer.

Becoming as you, a target in their gun sights,
all for addressing their wrongs, all for speaking of Rights.

Telling others to notice that the emperor's new clothes really aren't there,
that his highness's hind parts truly are bare.
Still, my question remains:
How could you dare?

Tigers' Stripes

I could not understand at first
how, from the early years since my birth,
others kept telling me how more was expected of me,
as if they had some divine knowledge of me and
what I could do on this Earth.

They were tigers all along. I know that now.
I have a half a life of experiences that has shown me how.

They knew. They saw those things in me.
They knew from experience all I could be.

They were tigers whose stripes I now recognize,
bearing similar markings of those who win the prize.
Having gained a deeper knowledge, I can now realize.

Man Mean

After the storms have passed and we can see beneath our layers,
After the forging of our metals and our heaven-toward prayer.

Man Mean will be no more,
This contrary cousin will be shown the door.

Man-Kind, the Good Being, the Gentle Soul shall emerge.
And with compassion and kindness, all negativity shall he purge.

Methodology

God made us unique by design, because He has a Perfect Mind.

Wanting us to learn to see the value of variety.

Splashing different colors, weights, and sizes;
giving different gifts and wondrous prizes.

Using His Universe to be as He sees it, making His Own doing it as He pleases.

Right Now You Are Perfect

Perhaps you have not yet realized it.

But don't give up, for you do have gifts.

You are perfect, right now, in this moment.

You are perfect in this place in this time

Just as you are.

Your spirit is the star that shines.

You are perfect, right now, in this moment of you.

You are perfect in this place in this time.

Funny Faces

If I want to make you laugh,
I will stand behind someone and mimic them when they talk to you.
And you will try to keep a straight face, just try, won't you?

Then when they turn toward me,
I will put on an innocent look, and you will try hard not to laugh or smile.
Knowing you'll tease me about it in a little while.

Pigeons

The pigeons in the park are dying, for now they have nothing to eat.
The people who used to feed them must now use that bread for meat.

The people say, "Blame the Government!"
The Government, "We work for you!"
The pigeons in the park are dying, so what are you going to do?

If We Wanted To

If we wanted to, we could change this world in our time.
We could make peace with each other, end wars and crime.

We are the beings who once lived in awe of the nighttime sky,
The very same star systems in which we now fly.

We have demonstrated the wonderful things we can do,
If we set our minds to it, if we wanted to.

If we wanted to, we could protect hearts pure,
Making every child's life safe and secure.

We could end all wars and start a love thing.
We could value our diversity and the gifts that variety brings.

Sure we could, if we wanted to.
We could do just about anything we set our minds to.

Sure we can, if we want to.
We can do just about anything we set our minds to.

Heritage Section

Dreamers

We Dreamers see past the horizon, knowing that day in our day will not be.
We dare to cast off these invisible chains of this tortured society.

And while the blood that is shed is ours, and it is our own tears which stain our faces,
We strive to make real our ancestor's dreams, and run our leg of the race.

Coretta

Tell them my time here was well spent,
And that after he was gone,
I tried to share what Martin meant.
I tried to carry the Dreams on.

There is always another way.
There is always a brighter day.

Speak to our thoughts against all war,
And tell them to make funds available for the poor.

Ask them to use America's wealth
To help the elderly and those with sickened health.

Beseech them to educate our young,
Showing the way of the Cross, not the gun.

Suggest that they will only learn to see the prize
When they look at things through God's Eyes,

Tell them my time here was well spent,
And that after he was gone,
I tried to share what Martin meant.
I tried to carry the Dreams on.

Assistance to a Brother in Need

Hold still, Dear Brother, and let me assist you now.
And while I do, I will tell you how.
We came from a place of beaches golden and winds sweet;
Your mother, our mother, Africa.

Let me share with you the marvels of Timbuktu.
And of our ancestors who built the Great Pyramids.
Of cultures and histories and a people whose spirits speak to us this day
And whose blood is our blood.

I would listen with you to the Griot,
Hearing of ancient times and warriors and passionate kings and queens.
We would marvel and laugh at how some tried to teach the young lions
How to conduct themselves and to become leaders of the pride.

And we would cry, no doubt, as we spoke of how you came to be here.

Of how some of us sold us.
And some of us betrayed us.
And some of us are no longer with us.
For the journey of the Middle Passage for them meant
the end of their time on this plane of existence.

We would speak of confinement and atrocities beyond measure.
We would, because we must, so that we will fully understand the importance of
who we are now and where we are now and what we must do
now.

And I tell you these things, because once I was as you are now, wounded.

And I was found by one of our Brothers.

And he treated my wounds.
And while he did so, he told me of a place
Where the wind was sweet and the beaches golden;
Your mother, our mother, Africa.

Why Rosa Sat

She sat down because she was tired, like any person would be,
from being on her feet all day.
Not realizing that in her defiance, a Movement would be born in that way.

She sat down because she had paid her fare.
She had paid her fare; she had paid her fare and more.
And it was time to remove the "Whites Only" signs from Jim Crow's doors.

She sat down because God had chosen Rosa Parks to be the spark,
fanned by the flames of discontent.
She sat down because she had had enough.
Did they not understand what "enough" meant?

She sat down because this child, descendant of queens and kings,
Would no longer tolerate discrimination.
She sat down because a brave little sister sitting on a bus would help to change a
Nation.

Color-blind

You make like you can't see me even when I am right in front of your face.
Walk right past me as if I don't exist in this time and place.

Bump me and don't say "I'm sorry" or "excuse me"
Not even a "thanks" if I do something courteous for you,
just because I happen to be of a different hue.

I wish you were like God. I wish you were more kind.
I wish you were like God, because He is Color-blind.

Government Cheese

They have no problem with you doing what you please,
as long as you keep eating the government cheese.

Telling you to stay in the hood,
as if it is for your greater good.

Or saying they will improve the schools.
Do they take you for a fool?

What they are doing to folks like me and you
is storing us for display like caged animals in a zoo.

Don't believe me? Don't think it's true?
Just try doing something other than what they want you to do.

Just try doing something positive to ease
the burden and the weight of the government cheese.

What is Race?

But a space where folks try to put me while I am in this time
and place.
And who said I had to run it, live life like a sports car, taking the engine and try-
ing to gun it?

I'm rethinking certain aspects of you and of me.
To get to the place where I say I want to be; the best and fullest and most loving
form of me.

Let those who gonna trip on Race, do what they do in this time and place.
Just don't try to categorize me for quantification's sake, frontin' and skinnin' and
grinnin' for ignorance's outtakes.

My lineage is human, my origin planet Earth.
Is there truly anything more important about the type and place of my birth?

What is Race?
My face, my place, my space, my taste, my haste, my waste?
What is Race?

How Will You Answer Them?

Some day we'll meet our road-pavers and Maker,
And examine the record of all we've done.

And we will have to respond to questions such as
"What did you do with the gifts you were given?"

When you are asked, what will you say to the spirits of our ancestors?

Past Chant

In my times of stormy silence, the drumbeats begin anew.
The old folks, the Africans, start doing what they do.

Beginning again with their rhythmic pitter-patter and their soulful syncopation.
Reminding me how it was for them, during the so-called "birth" of this Nation.

Singing to my soul of what acts have been done, Brother to Brother.
Reminding me that Children of God must help each other.

And in my actions, I must add lyrics to their song,
that my children will practice civil rights and not racists' wrongs.

Making the future one that is as no other,
where God's children see beyond the veils of color.

Brighter Days

Their hopes seem brighter, now that we are stronger, because we are their hopes realized.

Surely their spirits smile down upon us.

"Lost a few battles, but won the war!" they shout, because we are their hopes realized.

"No more darkness; thank God for this day!!" they proclaim, because we are their hopes realized.

"Not where we wanna be ... not where we gonna be ... but thank God, not where we were!!!"

Because we are their hopes realized.

Leftovers

Black ain't bad.
Like that media-fed foolishness about "You can tell the good guys in the cowboy movies, because they all wear white."

Plenty of the so-called good guys turned out to be bad guys by the time the movie ended.

Seems to me it is not about the color of the container that counts.

It's the quality of the contents.

And when we who are here become those that are gone on from here, we leave the containers behind.

No Mo' Dozin'

Wake-up call, America!
It's the less fortunate on the line.
They say they have not heard from you, but they hear you are doing fine.

Wake-up call, America!!
The builders of this country would like to talk.
They say it is time for you to acknowledge them and stop saying,
"Take a walk!"

Wake-up call, America!!!
Hear the rumbling, like thunder, coming near.
It is the sound of millions who hunger, plus your heartbeat full of fear.

Wake-up call, America!!!!
Don't ignore, because they ain't going away.
Time to address all of your children; time for the Brighter Day!

Restless

Gittin' tired of livin' like dis.
Hunkered down and chained wit only the sweat of my brow to quench my thirst.

Ain't s'posed to be dis way.
One bleeds, the otha bleeds,
Like we bleeds when the whip hit our backs.

I bin wonderin' iffin my dreams is real,
Where I seen us not yet to come,
Doin' well iffin they don't forgit us,
Doin' bad iffin we ain't remembered.

Gittin' tired of livin' like dis.

The Opposite of Hate Is Indifference

Dedicated to Beah Richards

You don't work on you what was worked on you and then claim you succeeded.

All you have done, in those instances, is mimic the evil perpetrated upon you.

And in so doing, you become that which you hate.

The way you work it is this—you flat-out don't let it make you like them.

"Them" being anyone who does evil to you or others.

Remember this 'Rule of Three'; If they don't put food on your table, clothes on your back, or a roof over your head—
be indifferent to them.

Before I Was Anything

Before I was ever in existence, I was already something wonderful.

Before my mama's mama's mama's momma, before Eve and Adam, I was already something spectacular.

I am the blood of the slaves and the son of pharaoh.
I am the maker of the bricks and he who designed mysterious pyramids.

I am spiritual like Martin Luther King, I am resilient like Malcolm X, I am strong like Rosa Parks, I am dedicated like Coretta Scott King, I am determined like Paul Robeson, and I am intelligent like George Washington Carver.

I love and I anger; I feel and I desire.

I am now as I was ever.

Long Time Suffering

Before you begin to move to your destiny,
you must understand how you came to be.

You must appreciate the gifts our ancestors bring
and give due credence to our long-time suffering.

And when you are tired and can no longer keep the pace,
reflect on those who gave their all for ours, the human race.

They knew that ours would be a better day,
and that is how they endured challenges that came their way.

Before you begin to move to your destiny,
you must understand how you came to be.

Mirror Mine

What is this shell God has placed me in?
A lighter shade than some of my kin?

A constant reminder of where my ancestors have been?
What is this shell God has placed me in?

I'll ask when I get to heaven, when I get in.
I'll ask when I get to heaven, I'll ask Him then.

The Land of Tears

We speak of parents crying, at the losses of their new,
but I've looked beyond the sorrow and of joyous days, I've seen a few.

For I see the children dancing in a circle, singing loud.
They sing of joy newly discovered, in this land above the clouds.

Of hope and life and laughter, no more bullets piercing skin.
They've gone off to a higher calling, to be with their heavenly kin.

I see the children dancing.
Come look, I'll show you where.
This land of tears is forgotten, and the people have learned to care.

Benny and the Jets

Bumming-Ass Benny was not his given name,
but that is what they called him then,
standing there begging without any shame
as the liquor store customers went in.

Seem like he never knew nothin' or wanted anything more
than to stand and bum for money in front of the liquor store.

But I saw him stand and salute one day,
As some planes flew by.
Brother even had a sad look on his face and tears in his eyes.

I heard later that he did that sometimes, because it made him think of when
he was a pilot back in the Korean War, one of a few good men.

Black Angels

Dedicated to the Tuskegee Airmen

Soaring to new heights,
Changing history with their might.
They flew in day and through dark of night,
For civil folks to do what was right.

Black Angels,
boldly holding destiny's charge to you,
taking your turn at the race of men,
and doing what you had to do.

Can any other than you know of your pain?
Or of how, time and time again,
you had to go against the grain
of America's so-called fruited plain?

Black Angels,
boldly holding destiny's charge to you,
taking your turn at the race of men,
and doing what you had to do.

The People

They wondered what was going on back when
the field slaves stopped their work, and then
they looked up and saw how, one by one,
the little slave children bore wings and were gone.

Their eyes smiled smiles of free souls that day,
and the ones who did likewise were heard to say,
"The people, the people, the people can fly!"
And to this day, the slave masters keep wondering why.

Now the overseers toil in their own fields,
but still look to the sky,
shaking their heads in amazement,
of how the people could fly.

Directions

Dedicated to my Brother Cedric

Our paths went away from each other.
Why were we so different, My Brother?

We came from the same place, and lived in the same space.
But went in opposite directions and ran a different race.

They Still Believe

They still believe, the little ones do, that no harm will befall them.
They still see themselves as precious among the race of men.

The most important lesson we need to teach them is to hold on to their love for us and for each other,
to care for each as Sisters and Brothers.

They still believe, though we give them cause to doubt by our actions.
They still believe, though we divide into factions.

They still believe, possessing hearts of gold.
They still believe, their precious spirits so bold!

They still believe,
they still believe,
they still believe,
in Love.

Nat Like Me

Me like Nat
Nat like Me

Neither of us bearing any injustices we see
Both being what we are destined to be

Knowing only that

Me like Nat
Nat like Me

Love Section

Rowing the Boat Slowly

I only walk it like I talk it; strong and true.
Gentle when a gentleman is needed and straight up when such a man is due.

Taking my me and exploring all of you, hoping that you want to take this journey too, with me, with you.

Finding me to be someone with whom you can explore all those hidden parts of yourself.
Those aspects of your sensuality left too long on the shelf.

I only walk it like I talk it; deep waters that bear the tide, rowing your boat past the middle of the lake, and back from the other side.

Wanna Soar?

Wanna soar and see what I have in store for you and me as we fly?
Wanna try?

Wanna sing about this wonderful and new and fresh and exciting and make-you-
wanna-do-the-Ooh-Ooh thing?

Wanna dance, have some romance perhaps take a chance
on a new position or new stance that will make a lady prance,

So your girlfriends will be jealous,
your co-workers curious,
and your kitty-kat purring at the sound of my voice!

Seasons of the Dance

She spots him from across the room, standing there looking fine.
He drinks in the vision of loveliness that she presents, thinking, "She will be mine."

And all else disappears in this place, that their attraction creates,
And the seasons of the dance begins, that true lovers can appreciate.

They move towards each other, sparks flying before hands meet, their gentle gestures attempting to hide passions, and tastes of love's flavors and sweets.

Cue lights, cue music, open the delights of each other's store.
Man, Woman, sweet passion, who needs more?

They have learned to make the most of this wonderful time and romance,
As only those who know the steps and music can appreciate the seasons of the dance.

So much so that when these dances end, they have stored enough memories to savor until next the seasons of the dance begins.

Misty Morning Rain

Will you come with me again, into the misty morning rain?
That sheen of perspiration upon your skin after we have made love yet again?

When I watch your silhouette, as you slumber with me,
I am mindful that all that makes Love so true is dependent upon the love of a
woman such as you.
When you rest skin to skin with me, I delight in thinking of what more things
we can do.

My Love, dare I stir you from your sleep into an embrace that you will remember
as the most erotic of sweet dreams?
A place of stars exploding, cosmic movements, and passionate sunbeams?

Can I take you there again? Will you come with me, again,
into the misty morning rain?

What You Wanna Do?

Can a man get a chance to chill with you, an exclusive view for two, as in for me and for you?
What you wanna do?

Waiting for a season that I can use this reason to do some serious
pleasing, and cease and desist from the current teasing that we do,
me and you.

I present not a moment, but a movement.
Ready, willing, and able to take you from, to, and through all the places
you've always wanted to go to.
What you wanna do?

Remain in the realm of fantasy, pretending that you don't even think
of me, when you sit in the bubble bath and marvel at the thought of
we?
What you wanna do?

Towards the Twilight

Where was it in the night
That we made love under the light?

Before the dawn and after the midnight,
Somewhere between the dusk and the daylight.

Moving as moonbeams cascaded all around,
Hearts beating faster as we played on passion's playground.

Your soul's windows open to fully display
The marvelous mysteries you share only with me, as part of the games we play.

And we made love under the light.
There, in your bed, in the middle of the night.
And everything was wonderful and everything was all right as we moved together
towards the twilight.

Take a Day ...

Take a day and spend it with me.
Take a day and see what we can see, see, see.

Hand me a note telling me what you'd like to do.
Hand me a note, and I'll go anywhere and do anything you want me to.

We both have been there flying solo and fantasizing so much.
Keeping our thoughts of us being together to ourselves while thinking of such
and such.
Knowing what we need is each other's touch.
Am I going there again, am I saying much too much?

Pump the brakes you say, and I smile.
I can pump them alright, but let me hit the accelerator for a while.
Turn on your radio and tune to my station.
Let me make your complete satisfaction my total dedication.

Take a day and spend it with me.
Take a day and see what we can see, see, see.

Nina Mosely

Would you call out my name if your passions I did inflame?
And if the love we made was always sweeter, was never the same,
Would you call my name?

When you, sensual and tender, are touching me,
Your strong defender of your right to not remain silent,
When we do the dance of no shame, would you call my name?

Sweet scents, tasty textures, fantastic feelings as fantasies become realities.
We ride the crests of the waves we create as they splash upon distant shores,
Making you smile as you know you will get more of what I have in store.
Wasn't that your plan when you let me in your door?

On the sofa, leaning over the chair by the stairs, in the walk-in closet, we go.
Inhibitions undone as clothes are shed and I bring down your walls of Jericho.
Want to see my trumpet again? Want to have another go?

And ain't this the way we both wanted it to be?
Am I right or what, Ms. Nina Mosely?

Toward the Midnight Sun

Was that the brightness of the day?
Or did the smile of your heart make the darkness melt away?

Illuminating and elaborating on you,
Queen of the Nile, Cleopatra, and Nefertiti renewed, in my arms.
Sparking passions and fantasies alike as I am honored to again sample your charms.

Making me see clearly, quenching my passions' thirst.
Showing me greater appreciation of such pleasures, perhaps for the first.

My wisdom of women gaining even greater ground,
As you walk me through your garden to your sacred ground,
The only place where the truest of treasures may be found.

Seeing the softness of your eyes, towards the warmth of your smile, I run.
To again bask in the glow of your essence,
And toward the midnight sun.

Guess When She Knows

When she first sees you, she makes up her mind.
You are a "lover-to-be" possibility, or,
Told to go to where you see the sign for her "be a friend" line.

She will or she won't. She'll do or she don't.

And there, my friend, is your true quandary; waiting to find out what she
Said you'll be and hoping that you are in the right category.

Place a Kiss on the Wind

Place a kiss on the wind, and let it glide from your lips to mine.
Let me drink from your vintage, love's sweetest wine.

Warming me as the summer breeze, knowing it is you that I long to please.
Taking me from where I am to where you are, from my distant planet to your
shining star.

Hold it for a moment, do you feel me there?
Has my invitation for passion made its way across the air?
Should I ease a little closer, would you like me there?

At First Sight

From the moment I first saw you I knew what we could do.
I could sense what you'd be like when a man loves you.

I could tell from the smile in your eyes.
I could sense how you would respond, you see.
I knew it would be like this if you took a chance to be with me.

I could smell your sweet scent, the most attractive of perfumes.
Your intellect becoming my aphrodisiac, as it calls me from across the room.

So I have loved you, My Dear, in so many ways that no time erases.
Moving with you in my most erotic dreams, making love in exotic places.

Thinking of you and what we will do.
And hoping from A to Z, and head to toe, and back to front, and heart and soul,
to get a chance to show you what I knew we could do, from the moment I first
saw you.

Change of Seasons

Didn't I find the time to give you all of the heart and body and soul that was mine?

Didn't I remain there through weather foul and fair, letting you know with action and words that I care?

Knowing you could do what you now do at any time and any place,
making your move away from me so you could have your "space."

So I gave my all to you, really, I gave my all.
Still somewhere, somehow, for some reason, our summer love gave way to the fall.
Guess what we had was a seasonal thing and not a love of a lifetime after all.

Genesis

I see your tears run down your face in your reflection in the window,
though your back is turned to me.

And you wonder, like I wonder, how it all came down to this.
It started, Dear Heart, with a kiss.

A gentle touching of our lips, and you were hooked, you just knew.
And you had to have another and another and received such as our love grew.

And these led to great times of sunshine and of rain,
Of joy of the inner woman and the heartache of love's pain.

Then led to this time, this place, this space.
Where we must decide if we are to go on or let go of this love of a lifetime.
Where we must renew our efforts or finish love's race.

And you wonder, like I wonder, how it all came down to this.
It started, Dear Heart, with a kiss.

Hidden Talents

I hope to take the time to show you how you are.
To reveal to you the things I've seen in you, to you.

The warmth, the strength, the determination to pursue you dreams
Against the odds and the naysayers, who don't believe that you can achieve.

That such a quiet spirit, such as yours, can be so strong.

Flower

After the thawing of your sadness,
When the stubborn side of you allowed me in.

That's when our Love blossomed and reached up to catch the rays of the sun.

Gaining strength as it shouted to the world of its existence.
Gaining glory as its beauty became known.
Gaining fame as it spread its sweet scent across the skies.

I Know Who You Really Are

I think that only you can't see the fire and determination that you exude.
This dogmatic, stubborn urge in you that says: "Never mind! I'll do it myself!"

But I've seen and felt your fire.
And I'm impressed by not only what you've done but by what you will do.

Who are you trying to fool, lady?
You, the pussycat with the heart of a lioness!

Waking

Why are the really good things confined to the realm of the dreamer?
The sensual, romantic, all left to the whim of the subconscious?

I would awaken to a reality fostered by my dreams of you, of the scent that you leave on the pillows.

The essence of you that makes me sleep on your side of the bed when you are not with me.

I would awaken, waking you in the process.

Whispering as I bring you from the world that is your dreams, the world of the really good things.

I would awaken, wondering if I am still dreaming, because you are there with me.

Snow

The light of the fire dims in your presence,
Its warmth put to shame by your soothing and searing essence.

And outside more flakes are falling, mimicking our inhibitions.
And gradually we explore even more, savoring our conditions.

While we entertain ourselves with the big pillows and an oversized comforter—our allies on this wonderfully wintry day.
Taking our fantasies and making them realities and finding new pleasures along the way.

And outside, the wind blows in rhythm to our dances.
And inside, we explore serendipitous moments and chances.

I gaze into the essence of your spirit, losing myself and finding my peace in your eyes, your smile, your You and my Me.

Knowing no man has ever been so grateful for a chance to play in the snow, and none is more satisfied with love's serendipity, as me.

Exploration

I would love to explore you, all and then some more of you, to give a lady the intimacy that she has been due.

Softly, gently, and thoroughly going into, the first chapter of You, while knowing this is one book I will never fully get through.

Cover to cover, checking your pagination, adding my comments and taking notes, inspired by each situation.

My learning of your yearning for a man who can appreciate your sharing.
Your smile and delight and surprise at your own daring.
Souls baring, hearts daring, have the young ones envious and the old folks staring.

And you, do you want to, too?
Or am I just foolishly hoping and fantasizing of dreams come true,
as in me and you on an exploration for two?

Walking Among the Stars

How is it that just the thought of you makes my heart flutter so?
It seems to grow wings!
Lifting my spirit above this plane, strumming like a virtuoso on my heart's strings.

And I walk among the stars.

My mind, my me, you see, has been awakened and taken to the celestial.
This love, this passion from the first definition of you as "Extra Special."

And I walk among the stars.

Your alchemy making our chemistry as I become aware of you and your mystery.
Our love of a type that goes down in history.

The Warden of Things that Are Already Free

You think you have them in check, don't you?
Your passions, pleasures, fears, and desires.
You think yourself in control of these, your inner fires.

So you consider yourself in control, locking your feelings in a cell,
Like prisoners confined in a high-security jail,
Hoping that your security system won't fail.

Hoping that your security system won't fail.

But they get out sometimes, I've seen you when they do.
They get out and party-hearty, and you know this is true.

Until you round them up again and put them back in their cell,
Confining them like prisoners in a high-security jail.
Hoping that your security system won't fail.

Hoping that your security system won't fail.

Who you think you really fooling, lady? You or me?
Because I know your real identity:
You are the warden of things that are already free.

Melodious

Softly, whispering from the heart.
Extending invitations to all of the parts.
But where with such wondrous choices would a man start?

To get to know her, listen for her melody, appreciate her song.
When you realize that all that she does begins at her heart,
Your actions will rarely be wrong.

Gently strumming symphonic sounds,
Her emotions entering and mesmerizing you,
As all inhibitions ease to the ground.

To get to know her, move to the music of her,
And patiently await your chance,
As you come to enjoy how the tempo of her music lovingly dictates her dance.

Cocoon

There are places we can go and have been.
And now you say we cannot go there again?
And what of now, and what of then?
Has so much changed that the butterfly is going back into her cocoon again?

Your Spring has come and the winter of many winters is at an end.
Time for you to come out and soar, my butterfly, time for our journey to begin.

And so I watch the beauty of your flight from near and from afar.
As you gaze in wonderment at me, as in awe of some distant star.

These are places we can go and have been.
And now you say we cannot go there again?
And what of now, and what of then?
Has so much changed that the butterfly is going back into her cocoon again?

The Good Doctor

Let me make that house call, the one you've been asking about.
The one you think of when you think of me and all your inhibitions are out.

I'll bring my little black bag of instruments, the ones that you'll love for me to use,
As I implement the long-overdue procedures of passion with you.
Would you like that too?

You couldn't even call this practicing medicine,
because what I'd do with you, would all be the essence of perfection.
And we would wonder, perhaps aloud right then,
why did we wait so long for these specialized procedures to begin?

And I'll write a prescription for refills aplenty,
To make sure your heart and head and body never run empty.

Making every boo-boo you ever had feel better,
Bringing much-needed sunshine to my Baby's stormy weather.

I'm the Good Doctor, professionally trained just for you.
Let me make that house call, and I'll do just what you need me to.

978-0-595-42757-4
0-595-42757-X